Pray Now
2008

Daily Devotions for the Year 2008

Published on behalf of the
OFFICE FOR WORSHIP AND DOCTRINE,
MISSION AND DISCIPLESHIP COUNCIL,
THE CHURCH OF SCOTLAND

SAINT ANDREW PRESS
Edinburgh

First published in 2007 by
SAINT ANDREW PRESS
121 George Street, Edinburgh EH2 4YN

Copyright © Office for Worship and Doctrine, Mission and Discipleship Council, the Church of Scotland, 2007

ISBN 978 0 86153 386 2

British Library Cataloguing in Publication Data
A catalogue record for this book is available from the British Library

It is the Publisher's policy to only use papers that are natural and recyclable and that have been manufactured from timber grown in renewable, properly managed forests. All of the manufacturing processes of the papers are expected to conform to the environmental regulations of the country of origin.

Typeset by Waverley Typesetters, Fakenham
Manufactured in Slovenia

Contents

Vulnerable Relationships

Astonishing Relationships

Sacrificial/Oppressive Relationships

Unconditional Relationships

Preface

We have our beginnings in relationships. There is no point at which we are unrelated, to the fabric of creation or to those around us. And Holy Scripture not only affirms that, from the beginning (Genesis), but presents story after story of encounter and learning about what follows on such truths. For relationships are soured as often as they are blessed: human connectedness, and disconnectedness, is to be worked at.

Pray Now 2008 offers a sampling of how we may read some of these Scriptural resources. There is a gentle insistence that with Scripture before us, the reading task must engage us. As has been famously remarked, the books of the Bible read us as much as we read them, and the stories therefore are not so much long, long ago and far, far away as surprisingly relevant to our personhood. We do well to linger with the thoughts they evoke. Prayer, after all, is the readiness for God to communicate with us, and not simply time for us to do all the talking.

We are indebted to the writing team who have put together *Pray Now* 2008. We are all of us in relationships and we ought to be in relationships. There is a critical moral dimension here. Life does not stand still, and the paths we choose to follow may bring blessing or curse. How we conduct ourselves towards others is very obviously an arena of our influence. It makes a great deal of difference how we respond to those around us. I hope very much that the work of the contributors on the Biblical material here presented will furnish rich encouragement to all who will pray and read with them. Pray now!

PETER DONALD
Convener
Worship and Doctrine Task Group
2007

Using this Book and CD

Communication is often said to be the basis of any good relationship – after all, how many relationships would endure if there were no talking or listening?

The *Pray Now* Group have always written daily prayers and reflections to help deepen our relationship with God; written words that give a place to start when people feel they have no words of their own, or prayer activities that allow time to think – and space to listen – when the words just don't seem enough. We seek to open up the channels of communication with God.

For the second year, we have included a CD to complement the contents of the book. The CD has eight tracks, each introducing a different type of relationship theme, as found in the pages of scripture, followed by a reading of one of the daily prayers from that section. There is the option of using the book or the CD on some days or, indeed, both together. It is hoped that, once again, the CD may give an alternative medium for daily devotion or a more practical medium for those who cannot use the book for whatever reason.

The 31-day format gives structure and pattern to the month for those who like to move through Day 1 to 31 in a natural progression. Others may find they wish to choose a prayer from one of the eight sections, so they may use a different section each day or even just dip in and out of the book as they feel appropriate. Whatever is most helpful to you is recommended. Hopefully, however, the variety of relationships in life and in God's creation will be explored and, in that process, our relationship with each other and, indeed, with God will reach a new level of understanding and appreciation.

GAYLE TAYLOR
Convener of the Pray Now *Group*

Days of the Month

Humdrum Relationships

Reality – unyielding, stone-hard, *there*. Where we live, and what we have to work round. The *humdrum*. Teillhard de Chardin, that most polymathic of Christian thinkers, when he was a small child, is said to have picked up a stone, and held it in his hand, and been overwhelmed with its substance, its materiality, its *thereness*. Jacob, on the run from his brother's wrath, puts his head on a stone to sleep, and wakes up saying 'Surely God is in this place, and I knew it not …'

The humdrum is just *there*. It's where we usually are, what's – and who's – usually around us; it's what is so stupefyingly familiar that we can usually hardly do more with it than take it for granted. Yet if ours really is an *incarnational* faith – a faith that God clothed himself in the dancing patterns of atoms which make our bodies and all things we touch and feel and smell – should it really surprise us that an abyss of meaning can suddenly open beneath the humdrum? And if we can find meaning in these patterns, why not then in the patterns which bind life to life, in relationships and belonging?

HUMDRUM RELATIONSHIPS – MARY AND MARTHA

Martha, Martha, you are worried and distracted by many things …

~ Luke 10:41 ~

You know me, Lord, so well.
I have seen the depressing sinkful of dishes, and heard the laughter from the sitting room
Where the TV is; and I have wondered
How I got landed with all this to do. Again …
And sometimes, I've said so. Vociferously.

And I have done the dishes
In a quiet house, and my mind has fled
To some happy or sad thought, but something real, something urgent
That the rhythmic swish of the dishcloth in my hand has set free.
And I have started, as the water from the still-running tap
Spills out of the bowl, or jumped when, in my hand,
The cup runs over.

You know me, Lord, so well.
Sometimes I am Martha, with my worthy agenda
And my sense of being taken for granted;
My hectoring sense of all that needs done, that no one is doing,
That drives me to ginger up and chivvy along.
The humdrum has to be got through first.
Then comes the good stuff …
And sometimes it is given to me to be Mary.
To be grasped by a moment when eternity strikes down into time,
And time must yield.

Then the humdrum is charged with meaning,
And not just the meaning of its own flat demands.
For you, Christ, are here. Now.
Help me to grasp your presence. Now.
To 'Be still, and know that I am God …' Now.
Maybe the dishes can wait …

Readings

Genesis 28:11–22
Exodus 3:1–5
2 Kings 6:8–23
Luke 15:11–32
John 12:1–8
Luke 24:13–35

Prayer Activity

Sit quietly, and look at your surroundings. Just stop completely. Marvel at the fact that it's all *there*. Accept it as it is. Then, in a way that seems appropriate to you – greet the presence of Christ in this reality.

Prayer for the Church

Those who bring care and encouragement to people in any kind of need and who work and pray for a healthier society in which all may find fulfilment

especially the Social Care Council, CrossReach, and the staff of the various units it operates.

Blessing

May the God of Mary, the God of Surprises,
Open our eyes to see his unexpected presence,
And the God of Martha, God-with-us in the routine things,
Strengthen us daily to do our work with joy.

HUMDRUM RELATIONSHIPS – MARY AND ELIZABETH

In those days Mary set out and went with haste to a Judean town in the hill country, where she entered the house of Zechariah and greeted Elizabeth.

~ Luke 1:39–40 ~

Perhaps, Father, when first we set out on our journey of faith,
We thought we were saying 'Yes!' to something
That would make life different. Exciting. Constantly *alive* ...
And perhaps – God forgive us – *exempt*
From what ordinary life so often is.

Was ever a 'Yes!' greater than Mary's,
When she answered the angel, 'Let it be to me according to your word ... '?
And with her 'Yes!' she embraced –
A mother's life. The whole deal.
Pride, perplexity, vulnerability, anxiety, pain – yes, all that;
And so much that is just humdrum.
No exemption from the sheer messiness of incarnation,
And all that that big word might mean, for *God's mum.*

Where we cling to our illusions, Father, she dispelled hers.
Where we romanticise, Lord, she demythologized.
She went to talk to Elizabeth about being a mother. The *reality* ...

Help us, like Mary, to find the reality of Christ,
Where life is what life *usually* is:
     Doing what needs to be done, meeting needs that aren't ours;
     Little things, not exciting, not even very elevating,
     But scary in their sheer volume; more, we fear than we can cope with.

We thank you for a commitment to us so total, an incarnation so complete
That 'Immanuel', 'God-among-us', meant this for Mary;
Hours, days, weeks, years, of humdrum motherhood.
Where, Mary might well have wondered, would God be, in all of this?
Then, unborn John danced his recognition in Elizabeth's womb.
Then, she knew.

Readings

Genesis 12:1–3a
Psalm 131
Isaiah 7:10–14
Jeremiah 1:4–20
Luke 2:1–7
Luke 2:22–40
Philippians 2:1–11

Prayer Activity

Faced with something shatteringly new – in her case, motherhood – Mary went straight to someone who would know and understand this new reality. Who shares your reality with you? Who, just now, is asking you to share their reality with them?

Prayer for the Church

Those who speak on behalf of the Church and who attempt to demonstrate the relevance of the Gospel for our life in society and relationships

especially the Church and Society Council and the Scottish Churches' Parliamentary Office.

Blessing

May we be kept from looking for God
Where we expect him to be
So that he can find us
Where we actually are.

HUMDRUM RELATIONSHIPS – SARAH AND ABRAHAM

But Abram said to Sarai, 'Your slave-girl is in your power; do to her as you please.' Then Sarai dealt harshly with her, and she ran away from her.

~ Genesis 16:6 ~

Sometimes, Lord, we know,
There is an incredible harshness to day-to-day life.
Hopes, expectations, dangerous dreams,
Grind together and shatter; love turns to hate, people behave very badly.
Shards and sharp edges wound and lacerate.

Life can be like that.
We dare not idealise, especially not in the name of faith,
As though life had to be simplified to fit our small vision of you.

That you in your faithfulness and love
Are gracious where we are not –
Is this not the heart of our faith?
And if it is not, Lord, let it be.

Sarai was insecure; Abram was weak; this is how they were.
From spat to vendetta, was this the family of your exalted promise?
Is this soap opera really the story of your covenant?
Help us to turn the question round, Lord.
'Does God really love real people?'
'Can God really love unlovable people?'

Free us from sanitised versions of faith.
Free us from that sundering of God from human reality
That makes us censors of the story.
Free us from the dark suspicion
That you can only deal with the nice, respectable bits of us,
Or that God is prim and easily shocked.
Challenge us with your realism, That sees us as we are,
And deals with *that*.

Readings

Psalm 139
Romans 7:15–8:2
Matthew 9:9–14
Matthew 13:24–30
Luke 18:9–14
Luke 19:1–10
John 19:17,25–27 and 21:15–24

Prayer Activity

Take a mirror. Look into it. Who do you see? What do you know about who you see? Knowing what you know, can you love and accept what you see? Can you see someone whom God loves? Now visualise someone with whom you have difficulties getting on. See their face framed in the mirror. Ask the same questions. Bring the answers honestly to God.

Prayer for the Church

Those who study Christian teaching and doctrine, and encourage mission, worship and witness through resources, meetings and education

especially the Mission and Discipleship Council.

Blessing

May we know that we are known, through and through,
And, known as we are, loved and accepted.
May we accept, daily, more of the truth of what we are,
And grow to love and accept others for what they are
As God's love in Christ transforms us.

HUMDRUM RELATIONSHIPS – PETER AND DORCAS

So Peter got up and went with them; and when he arrived, they took him to the room upstairs. All the widows stood beside him, weeping and showing tunics and other clothing that Dorcas had made while she was with them.

~ Acts 9:39 ~

Into the community of the Resurrection,
Into the fabric of daily life,
Death has come.
Across the web of relationships,
A cold hand has brushed,
Tearing the fabric, sundering the weave.
The silver cord is cut.
Its power is brusque, violent, summary.
Death is real.

Her hands wove, and sewed, and stitched,
And her life was woven in with theirs.
Now they finger her work,
Remember her skill,
Touch what her hands had touched.
We do this, we of finite flesh and blood.
When death takes away, we cling to what we have left.

Into the torn web
Comes Resurrection.
Not at the edge or the end of life
But in its midst.
Gently mending what is torn and sundered,
Renewing, healing, consoling and transforming,
Reweaving, mending the fabric of belonging.
Its power is patient, intricate, painstaking.
Its power is love.

Whether we live, or whether we die,
We are the Lord's.
Knitted together by his love,
We are his living body.

We have no need to cling,
For we have been grasped,
And here, where death is real,
More real the life that conquers death,
That life we're called to live, each day.

Readings

Psalm 90
Ecclesiastes 12:1–7
Ezekiel 37:1–14
1 Corinthians 15: esp. 19–23,35–43
Mark 5:22–43
Luke 24:36–53
John 11:17–37

Prayer Activity

Eat a pleasant seeded fruit. Pick out a seed. Contemplate its packaged, inhibited life. Relinquish it to the soil somewhere. Imagine the life that can spring from it.

Prayer for the Church

Those who bear witness to the Gospel of Christ in the midst of God's people, in Word and Sacrament, those whose ministry as deacons assist people in living out the Gospel in daily life, and those who recruit, educate and support them

especially the Ministries Council.

Blessing

While the patterns of daily life hold unchanged,
May the presence of Christ transfigure them;
When the patterns of life are torn and disrupted,
May the life of Christ mend and heal them,
Where the patterns of daily life, once shattered, are remade,
May the resurrection of Christ be glimpsed
In and through them.

Risk-taking Relationships

When we read about some of the risks taken by Biblical characters in their relationships, we can sometimes distance ourselves from that kind of experience which seems so far removed from our daily living. After all, Esther and Moses risked their very lives in making their requests for their people; Chuza's wife and the Syro-Phonecian woman risked social condemnation and punishment for associating with Jesus. However, in these bold stories we remember that all relationships are risky and complex. There is always a delicate balance of the known and unknown and a need for the right amount of trust, mixed with open-ness. And so it is in the trusted relationship with God, for those in the Bible and for us, that risks break new ground and create life-giving possibilities.

RISK-TAKING RELATIONSHIPS – ESTHER AND THE KING

Now Esther was admired by all who saw her ... the king loved Esther more than all the other women ...

~ Esther 2:15,17 ~

Safety in a number but most loved and special,
No wonder Esther was admired, God!

Esther had influence and attention
As her outward appearance pleased.

How often do we wish for immunity in the crowd,
Yet special privileges
Because we know someone or someone likes us?

God, we know that revealing our inmost is risky
And when we know, like Esther,
That beauty is fleeting,
That favour is fickle
And real love is challenging,
Help us have the courage God.
Help us have:
The spontaneity to ask the question,
The passion to say what we need
And the honesty to admit who we are,
And bless us in today's bold step.

Readings

Mark 1:14–20 *Calling the fisherfolk*
Exodus 3:1–6 *Moses and the burning bush*
John 2:13–22 *Cleansing of the Temple*

Prayer Activity

> Open your diary or look at your calendar and reflect on the events and circumstances of the past week. Call to mind the decisions you had to make. Were any of them difficult? How did you decide? Did you try anything new or bold? Did you stick to what you knew and play safe? Where was God in these times?

Prayer for the church

Its mission partners working with churches overseas, sharing their lives and challenges, and all those who strive toe support efforts to reduce the crippling debt in the world which contributes to famine, and oppression

especially the HIV/AIDS project and World Mission Council.

Blessing

Dance as though no one is watching you,
Love as though you have never been hurt before,
Sing as though no one can hear you,
Live as though heaven is on earth.

Anon.

RISK-TAKING RELATIONSHIPS – MOSES AND PHARAOH

I have also heard the groaning of the Israelites, whom the Egyptians are holding as slaves, and I have remembered my covenant.

~ Exodus 6:5 ~

O that we could face all danger,
able to call down a miracle from heaven,
with calm certainty in your faithful protection,
keeping us unscathed from the laughter of Pharaoh.

Yet, may we risk believing in justice,
even when we cannot call down angel armies,
but find ourselves alone before Pharaoh's throne,
daring to risk everything,
in the proclaiming of your realm.

May we risk believing in truth,
even when the world twists and abuses it,
but find ourselves unprotected before Pharaoh's throne,
daring to risk everything,
in the confidence of your stand.

May we risk believing in love,
even when we can find no reason to do so,
but find ourselves fragile before Pharaoh's throne,
daring to risk everything,
in the chance of the cross being right.

May we risk believing in you,
even when the world laughs at our foolishness,
but find ourselves naked before Pharaoh's throne,
daring to risk everything,
because you have risked everything for us.

Readings

Exodus 3:1–14   *I am who I am*
Micah 6:6–8   *Act justly*
Matthew 5:43–48   *Loving enemies*
Acts 9:1–19   *The conversion of Paul*

Prayer Activity

Reflect on those who face a bigger enemy than themselves, an individual against a system or a voice against a crowd. You may be thinking of someone like Mahatma Gandhi, or better, some lesser known person. Pray for them.

Prayer for the Church

The Church as it takes shape in areas where there are special difficulties – social, economic or health related

especially for the work of the Priorities Areas Committee.

Blessing

May your footsteps be taken justly,
your words said kindly,
your life lived fully,
and God always by your side.

RISK-TAKING RELATIONSHIPS – CHUZA'S WIFE AND JESUS

… and Joanna, the wife of Herod's steward Chuza … and many others, who provided for them out of their resources.

~ Luke 8:3 ~

God, we know it's the lesser known ones
that often make the bigger difference,
who have to stand out further
and take the biggest risk,
like Joanna, the wife of rich Chuza,
funding a ministry with quite conspiracy
and greater danger;
a woman's passion that leads her to resource,
not the great things that bring applauds and sponsorship deals,
kudos and a name for themselves,
but the daily things,
like food,
like water,
and like wine and bread.

May the world bless those who at great risk,
provide the everyday needs for us:
those who work without security,
to grow our tea and coffee;
those who work without protection,
to grow our flowers and fruit;
those who work without freedom,
to grow our rice and grain.

Bless those children of Joanna,
who know the risk of the everyday,
that furnishes our needs and lifestyles,
and whose voices….

Reading

Luke 8:1–5 *Those who supported Jesus*

Prayer Activity

Make yourself a cup of tea. Think about the story of that tea, who brought it to your table, who produced it, cared for it, blended it, grew the leaves, harvested it, and who themselves may never have tasted it.

Prayer for the Church

Those who ensure that the local church is well supported and staffed and who take imaginative initiatives in mission and outreach where people live, work and spend their leisure me,

especially the chaplaincies in hospitals, education, industry, prisons and residential homes, and those who work in the task groups devoted to education and nurture, mission and evangelism engaging with a variety of challenges, both rural and urban.

Blessing

Today, may we hear in whispers your whole story,
in silence your cry for love,
and in the people we see, nameless and unknown to us,
your saints among us.

RISK-TAKING RELATIONSHIPS – SYRO-PHOENICIAN WOMAN AND JESUS

... it is not fair to take the children's food and throw it to the dogs.

~ Mark 7:27 ~

Was there silence while you took breath?
Was there hushed stillness as you turned to see?
Was there an epiphany in the time it took you to recover from the retort?
That woman was going where angels feared to tread
and she trod on your toes!

And thank you God that she did,
for who wouldn't face the greatest hurdle
if they thought it would bring good to a loved one:
her daughter,
my child,
their partner.

Thank you God for the risk-takers,
who teach us the length love is willing to go,
and the barriers love will not stop at,
and the line love is willing to cross.
May we be such risk-takers for you.

But your cross was beyond any risk we can imagine.
Thank you God that you are the ultimate risk-taker:
without a limit to the love you offer us,
without a barrier at which love will stop,
without a line beyond which love will not cross
for us your daughters and sons,
your children,
your partners.

In such risk-taking for us,
it is we who find the silence that takes our breath away.

Readings

Exodus 6:28—7:7 *Moses visits the king*
Mark 7:24–30 *The Syro-Phoenician woman*
Luke 9:21–27 *Jesus speaks about suffering and death*
Acts 10:9–16 *Peter's vision*

Prayer Activity

Fold a piece of paper in half and open it out again. What things would you like to do but cannot? What lines would you like to cross but find yourself hesitating. Think of those who have crossed lines for love's sake. Pray for them, and strength for yourself that one day you may follow them.

Prayer for the Church

Those who at all levels encourage and enable different braches of the Church to relate to and to learn from each other about the Gospel we share

especially those involved in ACTS (Action Together of Churches in Scotland) the Committee on Ecumenical Relations, the World Council of Churches, The Conference of European Churches, and the Churches Together in Britain and Ireland.

Blessing

May today take you one step further than you intended
and allow you to celebrate in finding God waiting there.

Relationships of Challenge

We are not usually comfortable with relationships that challenge. They sit in that uneasy place which requires us to look at our prejudices, asks us to change in some way, to redefine our understanding of God, ourselves and the world. We occasionally need to hear challenging words to move us out of our comfort zones. Likewise, we may also need the courage to challenge others, so that through conversation, encounter and exchange we may reflect and revise the way in which we live out being Christian in the world.

The relationships in this section remind us, that if we are to be God's presence in the world, then being agents of change may be what we are called to be and to do.

RELATIONSHIPS OF CHALLENGE – JESUS AND THE RICH YOUNG MAN

But when he heard this, he became sad; for he was very rich.
~ Luke 18:23 ~

When we make poor choices,
When we get caught up in unhealthy patterns,
When we yearn and pine for all that glitters …
God, help us see why that is not good.

When we feel sure we are right,
When we are self sufficient and self righteous,
When we are confident in health and wealth …
God, help us know that we are not God.

God inspire in us today:
Faith beyond pat answers,
Motivation beyond self promotion,
Love beyond words.
Give us this day, the courage to move
Beyond our backgrounds and conditioning,
Our sadness and our unwillingness
To find costly
But rich
Adventures with you.

Readings

Deuteronomy 8:1–3 *Not by bread alone*
Luke 8:4–8 *Listen if you have ears*

Prayer Activity

Hold in one hand the thought of all things of great wealth and importance to you and in the other hand hold faith, family and friends. Reflect on the balance between your two hands, what hand is easiest to open?

Prayer for the Church

The local councils of the Church where support is given and policies made

especially the Presbyteries, their Moderators and Clerks; Kirk Sessions and Session Clerks; Congregational Boards, Deacons Courts, Committees of Management and their officers.

Blessing

God beyond answers,
Lord beyond words,
Spirit beyond imagining,
Move us today.

RELATIONSHIPS OF CHALLENGE – ABRAHAM AND ISAAC

'Take your son, your only son Isaac, whom you love, and go to the land of Moriah, and offer him there as a burnt offering on one of the mountains ...'

~ Genesis 22:2 ~

If love is a good thing, why is it tested?
If family is so sacred, why is it hard?
If parenting is precious, why is it painful?

If you, God, always provide,
Why do we sometimes feel we will lose everything?

Thinking of Isaac; innocently asking
'Where is the lamb for the sacrifice?'
We offer our prayers today for vulnerable children
In our time, naïve and trusting.

Thinking of Abraham; following without question,
Acting without hesitation, strangely focused
We offer our questions, our doubts and discomfort.

Thinking of Jesus; your only son,
Given to die because you loved us so much,
Christ who asks us to follow in costly ministry –
We ask today,
What is the cost?
What are the sacrifices we are prepared to make?

Reading

John 3:16

Prayer Activity

Call to mind a relationship or situation where there is a lack of trust. Offer your concerns and your questions about this to God.

Prayer for the Church

Those involved in the building up and support of new churches in new communities *especially those working in New Charge Development and those seeking to develop the initiatives of the Church Without Walls Report.*

Blessing

God,
of immeasurable love
of family beyond convention
of trust beyond understanding
bless through Christ your given son.   AMEN.

RELATIONSHIPS OF CHALLENGE – JACOB AND ESAU

Two nations are in your womb, and two peoples born of you shall be divided;
one shall be stronger than the other, the elder shall serve the younger.

~ Genesis 25:23 ~

From the time they were in the womb, there was struggle.
From the moment there were two, there was rivalry.
Right from the start there was the challenge,
Who would be first? Who was the strongest?
Who could outsmart the other?

God, today we see how, even siblings whose lives begin together,
In humanity are hot on the heels of ambition and success.
Today we struggle with the thoughts that:
Parents often take sides,
Children can emotionally blackmail parents,
In-laws can make life miserable for families,
Brothers and sisters sometimes lie and deceive each other.

God, in the struggle of the story,
In the tangles of families,
In the complexities of relationships.
Help us know where real strength lies.
Help us find honest blessing in our relationships
today and always. Amen.

Readings

Genesis 25:19–34
Genesis 27

Prayer Activity

Genesis 26:38 says, 'Have you only one blessing?' As Esau asks his father this, ask yourself the same question. How many blessings do you have? Is there one you think you want so much so you are not noticing other blessings in your life?

Prayers for the Church

Those who encourage and assist congregations in the development and exploration of patterns of mission and congregational life appropriate to their own context

especially the Scottish Churches' Community Trust and the Parish Development Fund.

Blessing

Count your blessings name them one by one,
Count your blessings see what God has done,
Count your blessings, name them one by one,
And it will surprise you what the Lord has done.

RELATIONSHIPS OF CHALLENGE – JOSEPH AND HIS BROTHERS

What profit is there if we kill our brother and conceal his blood? Come, let us sell him to the Ishmaelites, and not lay our hands on him, for he is our brother, our own flesh.

~ Genesis 37:26–27 ~

God,
It's hard to know where abuse lies when there is a favourite in the family.

Favoured perhaps because of personality, intelligence, flair, the ability to please

Or are they
Arrogant, scheming, egocentric individuals who like the sound and feeling of
Me, me, me,
Mine, mine, mine,
Getting their own way?

And the rest,
Seeking their place in the pecking order,
Take turns in seeking attention.

Planning, plotting, imagining,
How much better life would be without the favourite.
Cruelty, envy, jealously, creep into the heart of the human soul
Stirring the passion of revenge

When all they really long for is for someone to notice they exist
And to show some pride in them.

God,
All of us in our way act out our longing for acceptance and worth
So when we carry the unease of our families
Remind us that in you
We are loved
We are valued
We are precious
We are of worth.

Readings

Genesis 37–46   *Joseph and his family*

Luke 15:11–32   *Parable of the Prodigal Son*

Prayer Activity

Look through some photos of your family. What memories do they hold? Good? Bad? Try to imagine why family members behave the way that they do and to see life from their point of view!

Prayer for the Church

Those who are responsible for the good management of the Church's financial resources and who labour to make its members aware of the meaning and implications of Christian Stewardship

especially the Stewardship and Finance Committee.

Blessing

Accepted and valued,
respected and affirmed,
loved and precious,
live, in the peace of Christ.   AMEN.

Relationships of Power

How shall we pray about power? We approach it with suspicion; isn't that what Christians are supposed to do? And perhaps we imagine that by forswearing power, refusing its seductions, we can soar, pure, above its conflicts and contestations, its ambition and aggression. And don't we then, in the very act, *seize the power* of the moral high ground, that does down our opponents so much more effectively than their own unsubtle, naked power-plays? Then there's victimhood. 'See how you have hurt me! See how my power – and dignity – have been taken away by you! And see how I take them back ...' Then there's *abdication* ...

And what does *real* powerlessness do to one?

Whether we forswear, or grasp, we are immersed in the currents of power. Through our words and actions, through our being in the world, it courses. As we are moved, pushed and pulled by it, so we exert – use – power ourselves. Inescapably. How shall we pray about power? By honestly mapping its flows in the great patterns of Scripture; in the relationships which let us explore it. We could start with Jesus' relationships in the Gospels; but here, we don't. You might do that, for yourself ...

RELATIONSHIPS OF POWER – AHAB AND JEZEBEL

He said to her, 'Because I spoke to Naboth the Jezreelite and said to him, "Give me your vineyard for money; or, if you prefer, I will give you another vineyard for it"; but he answered, "I will not give you my vineyard."' His wife Jezebel said to him, 'Do you now govern Israel? Get up, eat some food, and be cheerful; I will give you the vineyard of Naboth the Jezreelite'

~ 1 Kings 21:6–7 ~

I *want*, Lord. Don't we all?
And what I want is what I don't have.
Having does not kill the butterfly *Desire*.
It flits from what I have just got, to light on what I don't have. Yet.
Desire is, I know, insatiable. It empowers me,
Just as it empowers, charges, drives, this world of conspicuous consumption.
For I am a consumer, and the consumer is king.

My desire is not outrageous or brutal, Lord. Surely my desire kills no one.
It would be satisfied with very little more than I already have.
I could say 'Enough …' *Any time I wanted to.*

But I hear the seductive whisper
'Why settle for less?' 'You're worth it!'
I lip-know, but do not heart-know, that these things
Are no measure of who and what I am.
Not before You. But they are, with me.
And still the voices whisper.
'Are you not a consumer?' 'Is the consumer not king?'

'Is it my fault if the world works this way?'
Sometimes I can manage to say it and believe it.
If consumer society empowers the consumer,
And I happen to be a consumer …

Power is exercised in my name, Lord God, and I am complicit,
Because I am silent, and because I continue to consume.
My desire would consume the world.
Teach me how to decline, with proper revulsion.
Teach me what is *enough* …

Readings

Exodus 16:14–36
Amos 4:1–3
Luke 4:1–13
Luke 12:14–34
Luke 16:19–31

Prayer Activity

Take the phrase 'I couldn't live without it!' and dwell on it for a moment or two. What springs to mind? What couldn't you live without? Now – imagine choosing to live without it. Or having to. How would that be? What would that mean to you? Go back to the phrase 'I couldn't live without it!'. What do you think that actually means? Offer all of this to God.

Prayer for the Church

Centres to which people may withdraw to renew body and mind, to engage more deeply in worship and study, seeking the relevance of the Gospel for the contemporary world

especially Scottish Churches House, Key House (Falkland), Iona Abbey and the Macleod Centres and other interdenominational retreat centres.

Blessing

Let us so live
That what we want
Is what we need.
Let us so pray
That what we seek
Is what you want for us.

RELATIONSHIPS OF POWER – ELIJAH AND JEZEBEL

*Then Jezebel sent a messenger to Elijah, saying, 'So may the gods do to me
and more also, if I do not make your life like the life of one of them by this time
tomorrow.'*

~ 1 Kings 19:2 ~

You were too easy to see in the whoosh of flame;
On that mountain of vindication and *power* ...
Elijah had to unfind you, after that, in order to find you again.
Yet Jezebel trumped Carmel with just a death-threat.
Naked, corrupt, unbounded power. And totally credible.
Broken by power, Elijah fled. To a different mountain.

'What are you doing here, Elijah?' On Horeb ...
Out it all pours. 'I was faithful, I made a stand, it was all going so well!
And now they seek my life, to take it away.'
And what's unsaid. 'I need power to countervail power. I need God.'

Earthquake, lightning, storm-wind; minatory, dazzling, *power aplenty.*
But God isn't there. Power just isn't where God is. So where is God?

And then – *the sound of nothing at all ...*

Same question – 'What are you doing here, Elijah?'
The answer – completely different. *Yet word for word the same.*
Yet everything really is different.
Jezebel, and her power, and her pomps, are still there,
But Elijah goes back. Suddenly, he can face it.
Now he knows where God will be. There ... *Just* ... *there.*

I open my eyes from prayer – did I miss something, Lord?
How, when nothing has changed, has everything changed?
How, when I turn from the assurances of power,
Having failed to find you there,
Do I find you in the stillness of my own acknowledged powerlessness?

Readings

I Kings 18:17–40
I Kings 19:1–18
Psalm 46
Luke 9:28–36
Luke 22:39–44
John 14:27–9
I Corinthians 1:18–31

Prayer Activity

Listen to the silence – and acknowledge that it isn't actually silent. Acknowledge, one by one, the sounds it contains. Think about the difference between **silence** and **peace**. Offer the silence –such as it is – of real life in the real world to God. Ask him for peace such as the world cannot give.

Prayer for the Church

For those who ensure that the fabric of church buildings is maintained and that the Church's heritage in buildings is conserved for the good of the Church and nation

especially the General Trustees and the Committee on Church Art and Architecture.

Blessing

You have brought us here,
And here we are, for you,
And here you are, for us.
Let us return to the pattern of daily life
Knowing that everything will be the same,
Yet understanding that all things are different and new.

RELATIONSHIPS OF POWER – JOHN THE BAPTIST AND HEROD

And Herodias had a grudge against him, and wanted to kill him. But she could not, for Herod feared John, knowing that he was a righteous and holy man, and he protected him. When he heard him, he was greatly perplexed; and yet he liked to listen to him. But an opportunity came when Herod on his birthday gave a banquet for his courtiers and officers and for the leaders of men of Galilee.

~ Mark 6:19–21 ~

I often feel powerless, Lord. We all do. We say so all the time.
It feels like our usual condition in the world. Corks on a tide …
Often it is our excuse, and seldom does it convince us.
But still we feel powerless. *Really* powerless …

Yet even powerlessness can choose whom it empowers.
There is *always* a choice of masters.
John chose, and in imprisoned powerlessness
He spoke the painful, powerful truth.

Or we can be Herods, mesmerised by truth, even *painful* truth,
Longing for courage to vote it to power.
'The truth shall set you free …' – but liberation is a terrifying thing.
So John in chains was free, and Herod, enthroned, a captive.

Like Herod, we listen, and do not commit.
We empower, not truth, but our own captivity,
Our very disempowerment!
Fascination, blurred boundaries, compromise,
And we, too, are bound fast by blurted, hasty words.
Somehow – we missed the moment – our pledge has been extracted.

Show us the freedom we have, even in life's limitations,
To embrace the truth;
The power we have, even in our powerlessness,
To refuse to yield to power.
Show us the choice we have, when other choices have run out,
To choose the empowered powerlessness of the prophet
Over the finite power of the power-brokers.

Readings

Daniel 3:1-28
Daniel 6
Amos 7:10-17
Luke 18:1-8
John 19:1-16

Prayer Activity

Review the situations in your life in which you or someone else experience powerlessness. Which of them does Herod's situation cast most light on? Which John's?

Prayer for the Church

Those involved with Christian counselling and healing

especially the Christian Fellowship of Healing and local groups in your area.

Blessing

May we be blessed with a gentle, humble courage of truth
Courage enough to *choose*,
Courage enough to *speak*,
Courage enough to *live*
The truth as you show it to us.

RELATIONSHIPS OF POWER – SARAH AND HAGAR

Abram said to Sarai, 'Behold, your maid is in your power; do to her as you please.' Then Sarai dealt harshly with her, and she fled from her.

~ Genesis 16 ~

Power, for us, is such a tricky business.
We ascribe it slickly to you – *God of power and might* –
And instantly you challenge us,
Revealed in the flux of worldly power
As the powerless, crucified God.

But power, and who has it, still shapes our relationships – our lives.
We expertly read its flows, its peaks and troughs.
A shake of filings on a sheet of paper reveals the field of a magnet.
A sprinkling of people in a story
Reveals to us the field and play of power.
We are not innocent, or naïve, where power is concerned.

It is Sarah's house; she writes the rules, sets the emotional thermostat.
That is power! The power to make life hell – albeit from sheer insecurity.
Hers is the present, and hers the long past with Abraham.

But pregnant Hagar is tomorrow,
And Hagar has the power of the weak,
And knowledge of the secret, hurting spot.
She knows where to press. . .

Abraham, the man, pathetic in his formal power.
He cannot placate or console Sarah. He cannot protect Hagar.
He simply abdicates.

The flux of life, the ebb and flow of power, shape our relationships.
We need faith, to be able to entrust to you
Those we love but cannot protect.
We need love enough to love
Those who can absorb all the love we give, and still need more.
We need strength, to be able to stand, gently, against power.
We need courage, to absorb hurt, and break the cycle . . .

Readings

1 Corinthians 13
Philippians 2:1–11
Romans 4:1–9
Galatians 5:22–26

Prayer Activity

> Take an object – a small stone, a nut, a ball – which fits in your clenched fist. Grasp it as hard as you can. Imagine someone is trying to take it from you. Resist them for a few seconds. When you are quite clear that it is your choice to do this, choose to open your hand, and offer the object. Now, when you are ready, and it is your choice, put the object down – right out of your hand. Relinquish it. Feel the power of offering and giving, over the power of seizing and grasping.

Prayer for the Church

Those on the margins of society, the poor, the powerless and the vulnerable *especially the Safeguarding Committee and its team of staff and volunteers.*

Blessing

God make us strong
To stand for the right;
God make us strong
To speak the truth;
God make us strong *enough*
To lay aside power,
To embrace weakness,
To break the cycle
In the freedom love gives.

Vulnerable Relationships

All relationships carry a certain amount of vulnerability but we tend to associate vulnerability more with people who need our special care - those who are sad, lonely, bereaved, hurting or in pain. There may be times in our lives when we too feel more vulnerable, and look to the care and comfort of others to feel God's presence near us.

Vulnerability is often associated with weakness or helplessness. It is seen as the soft option of a relationship. If we are vulnerable we feel exposed and risk being hurt. Yet the paradox of vulnerability is that is carries great strength. An inner strength that emerges when we acknowledge our deepest need for God.

The vulnerable relationships in this section articulate something of this need for God especially at times when our prayer life seems empty or we struggle to glimpse God's presence near us. But they also show us something of the essence of humanity – that being vulnerable, being reliant on another, was how God was first revealed as human. It may be that vulnerability is a trait we need to be more open to in our daily lives, not just at the times when we are feeling low or in need. In doing so we open ourselves up to a silent and often unseen strength and power.

VULNERABLE RELATIONSHIPS – JOB'S COMFORTERS

Then Job answered: "I have heard many such things; miserable comforters are you all. Shall windy words have an end? Or what provokes you that you answer? I also could speak as you do, if you were in my place; I could join words together against you, and shake my head at you ... If I speak, my pain is not assuaged, and if I forbear, how much of it leaves me?"

~ Job 16:1–4,6 ~

Her reality challenges my faith
Because it will not fit it
Neatly.
His universe, where he must live,
Challenges my faith
Because it is bigger than my cosy little God.
Your pain challenges my faith
Because it is deeper than my consolations can reach.

So I turn from encounter to exhortation,
And I exhort only – and desperately –
Myself. I comfort – only myself ...
If only I could listen, and forgo my own comforting speech.
If only I could bear with all that must be told,
And just sit there and hear it.

O for a ragged faith,
Torn and slashed by reality,
Frayed from embracing things as they actually are,
And not understanding!

O for an angry faith,
That searches for God in what is, and not in what I wish were there.
O for an inconsolable faith
That will settle for nothing less than God.
O for a ruthlessly honest faith
That censors nothing for consolation's sake.
Bring me, bring us, to the point of true consolation
Where truth and faith coincide.

Readings

Job passim, but especially
chh. 4:1–7; 5:8–27; 7:16–21; 8; 9; 10; 11; 12:1–5; 42:7–9, 42:10.

Psalm 22

Psalm 137

Luke 22:40–6

Mark 15:33–40

John 20:24–5 only

1 Corinthians 1:17–25

Prayer Activity

Visualize someone you know quite well. It could be someone who is going through a hard time at the moment, but needn't be. In the imagination of prayer, just 'sit with them', and *listen to them*. Although they aren't there 'in the flesh', see if *attending to them* doesn't lead you to understand what you already know in a different, and deeper way. Don't interpose any of your own thoughts, or your ideas about what things are like for them. Just consider carefully *what comes from them*. Then try opening up to God, who sits with you and listens to you, and attends to you. Don't censor anything. Tell God how you feel.

Prayer for the Church

Those in my own congregation, assisting it to be part of the living witnessing Body of Christ in the world.

Blessing

Goodness and mercy,
Light and life,
Comfort and joy
Be yours through Christ our Lord.

VULNERABLE RELATIONSHIPS – JESUS AND SIMON OF CYRENE

As they went out they came upon a man from Cyrene named Simon; they compelled this man to carry his cross.

~ Matthew 27:32 ~

Jesus at your most broken and vulnerable
a stranger came
and took up your cross
holding the weight, easing the burden and pain.

So we too pray for that presence in our lives
when the knocks of life seem hard to bear
and the accompaniment of someone near
just might make the difference.

We pray:
    For those in debt
    who panic about where the money for the next bill will come from.

    For those who are unemployed or facing redundancy
    who need to hear an affirming 'Yes! You are chosen.'

    For those who are ill in mind, or body or spirit
    who need to feel a tender healing presence

    For those who are lonely
    who ache for human companionship

    For the elderly waiting…

    For those who are experiencing a breakdown in relationships
    who need to believe again in the potential to love

Come close to all Lord who need help with the burdens of life
Come carry the load
Come ease the pain
Come and be a presence alongside us.

Readings

Psalm 42   *Psalm of Lament*
Psalm 68:19–20   *Psalm of thanksgiving*
Matthew 11:28–30   *Jesus bears the burden*
Galatians 6:1–10   *Bear each other's burdens*

Prayer Activity

Write down some of the burdens that you are carrying. Burn the paper over a candle or throw it away. Give your burdens over to God and be free.

Prayer for the Church

Those who care for members of the armed forces as they seek to preserve peace in the world

especially the Committee on Chaplains to Her Majesty's Forces.

Blessing

Lord Jesus
When we carry a heavy load
May you accompany us in our sorrow
And give us the strength to carry on walking the way of your kingdom.

VULNERABLE RELATIONSHIPS – HAGAR AND GOD

Abram said to Sarai,' Your slave girl is in your power, do to her as you please.'
The Sarai dealt harshly with her, and she ran away from her.

~ Genesis 16:6 ~

O Holy One
Present in our despair

When relationships turn sour,
Become complicated, jealous or abusive.
You come close in the weeping.

When there is no one to turn to,
No way out of a situation, other than to walk away,
You come close in the weeping.

When life is dry and barren
And we are lost and lonely in the desert.
You come close in the weeping

When a parent reaches rock bottom
And cannot even bear the crying sound of their child.
You come close in the weeping.

Be a comfort and a guide
A light in our dark places.
'Do not be afraid,' you say to the cries of our distress.
Come Lord,
Come close
Come close in our weeping.

Readings

Jeremiah 20:7–18   *Jeremiah denounces his persecutors*
Mark 5:22–43   *Jesus healing ministry*
Luke 23:27–30   *Women of Jerusalem weep for Jesus*
John 11:1–43   *Death of Lazarus*

Prayer Activity

'I am sometimes more aware of God on Good Friday, than I am on Easter Sunday.' Think of the times when you have been at your most sorrowful – how has God's presence been revealed to you. Do you feel God close to you? Spend some time thinking abut the people today who need to feel God's presence is with them.

Prayer for the Church

The Church as it meets in council and assembly and those who plan for and resource its meetings

especially the Assembly Arrangements Committee, the Moderator of the General Assembly; the Principal Clerk and the Depute Clerk.

Blessing

In weeping, God is with us
In despair, God is with us
In silence, God is with us
Come close,
God be with us.

VULNERABLE RELATIONSHIPS – JESUS AND CHILDREN

Truly I tell you, whoever does not receive the kingdom of God as a little child will never enter it.

~ Mark 10:15 ~

Jesus,
children ran towards you and you welcomed them with open arms
reprimanding those who wished to keep them under control.

We have lived as children, and have grown up leaving behind something of the
trust,
enthusiasm,
vulnerability,
curiosity,
imagination,
openness,
acceptance,
the playfulness of childhood.

We too often reprimand children,
'They don't behave.' They're too noisy.'
And yet we want children to be present –
'They are the church of tomorrow!'

Jesus you call children to be part of the church
not because they are church of tomorrow
but
because the Holy Spirit speaks through them today
because they remind us of the essence of our humanity
because they invite us to become again the child we once knew
because we need to be like them
trusting,
enthusiastic,
curious,
imaginative,
open
accepting and playful
to enter into the kingdom of heaven.

Readings

Psalm 8:1–2   *Psalm of human dignity*
Exodus 2:1–10   *Baby Moses*
1 Samuel 3:1–41   *Call of Samuel*
Matthew 18:1–7   *Jesus teaches about children*
Matthew 19:13–15   *Jesus blesses children*
Luke 2:41–50   *Birth of Jesus*

Prayer Activity

Do something playful and childlike this week – enjoy the experience and give God thanks for it!

Prayer for the Church

The organisations of women and men who worship, study and reach out to others *especially the Church of Scotland Guild.*

Blessing

Renew me with curiosity, so that I may learn more of myself and the world.
Remind me to play, so that I can hear your laughter.
Inspire me with vision, so that I can live this day with passion for your kingdom.

Astonishing Relationships

There is always something subversive about a relationship that speaks about renewal and new life, and many of the Biblical friendships we read about speak in just that way. Astonishing they are; but that description doesn't seem to do them justice, for in those relationships, actions break open the wiles of heaven. An ostracised Samaritan woman offering a strange foreigner a drink is indeed the way heaven works – for how many sensibilities does that action break apart? Or two geriatrics who recognise in the youngest child the whole promise of heaven – how many prejudices does that shatter? Or a tax collector sharing a meal and then a future with the one who called him down from the tree, back 'down to earth' – how many cultural norms does that defy? It is always a dangerous liaison when you get involved with heaven, for the outcome can be a confessing and redeemed tax collector or an accepted and renewed Samaritan woman or the presence of resurrection round a table, and these things in anyone's language … are astonishing.

ASTONISHING RELATIONSHIPS – DAVID AND JONATHAN

... the soul of Jonathan was bound to the soul of David, and Jonathan loved him as his own soul. Then Jonathan made a covenant with David, because he loved him as his own soul.

~ 1 Samuel 18:1,3 ~

O Lord my God, I will give you thanks for ever
That my heart sings for my beloved
My deepest soul friend
In whom my spirit delights

Formed in a covenant of love
A touching closeness
Not fuelled by lust or desire
But treasured with deep tenderness
In union, in communion
With God and each other.

O Lord my God, I will give you thanks for ever
That my heart sings for my beloved
My deepest soul friend
In whom my spirit delights

When the years are silent
Separated by time and space
Meeting again seems only like yesterday
For in you I am more fully alive
More fully human
More me

O Lord my God, I will give you thanks for ever
That my heart sings for my beloved
My deepest soul friend
In whom my spirit delights

A love unspoken which when death parts
Comforts the mourning family
But speaks not to the aching grief in the closeness of friends.

O Lord my God, I will give you thanks for ever
That my heart sings for my beloved
My deepest soul friend
In whom my spirit delights

Readings

Ruth 1	*Ruth and Naomi*
John 19:25–7	*Mary and John*
Acts 13:14	*Barnabas and Paul*
Acts 15:37–41	*Paul and Silas*

Prayer Activity

Think of your friends and list the attributes you like best about them. Give God thanks for friends and think about what it is that you give to them.

Prayer for the Church

Those who seek to renew the life and mission of the Church and establish its priorities for its future witness to the Gospel

especially the Council of Assembly.

Blessing

Blessed be those who are loyal and faithful
Blessed be those with who make us fully alive
Blessed be the name of a friend

ASTONISHING RELATIONSHIPS – WOMAN AT THE WELL AND JESUS

A Samaritan woman came to draw water, and Jesus said to her, 'Give me a drink.'

~ John 4:7 ~

Loving Jesus, in our misunderstanding,
meet us.
Loving Jesus, in our secret lives,
meet us.
Loving Jesus, in our solitary living,
meet us.

Meet us with the full force of heaven,
gently,
with a grace-filled moment and a living word,
that speaks into all living deserts:
the dryness of our relationships,
the barrenness of our community,
the solitariness of our culture
to every woman enslaved,
to every asylum seeker turned away,
to every child abandoned.

Water these deserts,
not just with water,
but with living water,
that each may never thirst again,
that this world may never thirst again.

Loving Jesus, in our thirst for connection,
within a community disconnected,
may we pass the cup abundantly
and with reckless generosity.

Readings

John 4:1–30   *The Samaritan woman at the well*
Luke 4:16–21   *The community of God's realm*
Acts 2:43–7   *Life of the early community*
Numbers 20:1–13   *Water from rock in the desert*

Prayer Activity

Place a cup of water before you. Reflect on it, how it gives life and how it can equally harm with disease and flood. Give thanks for its life-giving properties and pray for those affected by the harm it can bring. Drink the water and hear Jesus words to us: I am the water of life.

Prayer for the Church

Those who bring their creativity to bear on making known the Church and the Gospel in print, news media, sound and website

Blessing

May God fill every cup you drink
with life and eternity
in equal handfuls.

ASTONISHING RELATIONSHIPS – ANNA AND SIMEON

... or mine eyes have seen your salvation, which you have prepared in the presence of all peoples ...

~ Luke 2:30–31 ~

There is subversion
in waiting,
in the tenacity of those who hope
and dare to long
for revelation,
for justice,
for truth.

And subversive beyond that
is when old eyes recognise,
fulfilled in a newborn,
the hope they have been harbouring for generations.

May we see in each new generation,
the evolving of the world,
in lives that will carry on our story,
with the chance for a new revelation of Gospel.

The subversion of old age,
is the placing in each younger generation,
the ongoing story of faith,
and the whole hope of the Gospel.

May we recognise what is good to pass on,
and the right time in which to pass it.

Readings

Luke 2:25–38   *Simeon and Anna*
Ecclesiastes 3:1–8   *A time for everything*
Ecclesiastes 12:1–5   *Remember old age*
Job 32:6–10   *Not only the old are wise*

Prayer Activity

Spend some time considering words of parents and grandparents you remember years after they have been spoken and how they have revealed wisdom to you. How has what a previous generations said, shaped you? What has been wise and what needed to be left behind? What has been unwanted baggage and what has influenced you in the direction of your life?

Prayer for the Church

Those who work with young people, with patience and imagination, demonstrating the truths and principles of the Gospel in and through fun, laughter, discussion and debate

especially the work of the Youth and Children's Assemblies.

Blessing

May God let you see what others miss:
promise cradled in every wonder,
the flow of life shaping a sacred story,
where you, and love, dance together daily.

ASTONISHING RELATIONSHIPS – EMMAUS AND STRANGERS

When he was at table with them, he took bread, blessed and broke it, and gave it to them. Then their eyes were opened, and they recognized him; …

~ Luke 24:30–31 ~

May we gather round table
as strangers,
yet in the sharing of bread,
discover we are sisters and brothers.

May we look into the eyes of travellers
as strangers,
yet in the sharing of a word,
discover we are companions on the road.

May we hear the confusion of journeyers
as strangers,
yet in the sharing of questions,
discover we are adventurers on the way.

Jesus, who meets us in the guise of stranger,
whose face is glimpsed in breaking open hospitality,
create among us
countless meeting places:
in setting of table,
in opening of doors
in sharing of food
in offering greetings
that we meet you
in every stranger,
and in this sharing of Gospel,
discover our own place in the family of God.

Readings

Luke 24:13–35 *Emmaus experience*
Acts 9:1–9 *Damascus Road Experience*
Mark 7:24–30 *Syro-Phoenician woman*
Acts 10:9–16 *Heaven's inclusive picnic*

Prayer Activity

Place an empty chair in front of you. Image it is Jesus sitting there. What do you want to ask him? And what does he say?

Prayer for the Church

Those who care for the interests of those who are retired and in need of support *especially the Church of Scotland Pension Trustees and the Housing and Loan Fund.*

Blessing

May eating together always make more sense than fighting,
may sharing what we have always make more sense than taking,
may asking our questions always make more sense than shouting our certainties,
and may breaking bread together always make more sense than division.

ASTONISHING RELATIONSHIPS – ZACCHAEUS AND JESUS

When Jesus came to the place, he looked up and said to him, 'Zacchaeus, hurry and come down; for I must stay at your house today.'

~ Luke 19:5 ~

When we feel we are unimportant and not noticed
You see in us the potential and possibility we fear to live up to
You surprise us with an unexpected,
'I choose you.'

When our wealthy lives are lived out at the expense of the poor
You encourage us to be uncomfortable with our extravagance
You challenge us with an unexpected,
'I choose you.'

When we worry that our bodies may be too fat or too small
You see that which is deep within us and beyond the external
You affirm us with an unexpected,
'I choose you.'

When the lives we lead or decisions we take, make us unpopular
You demand we seek Justice and act with mercy
You change us with an unexpected,
'I choose you.'

So come amongst
the lonely
the small
the wealthy
the unloved
the unpopular

Come
and be the guest of a sinner
that by choosing us,
meeting us,
being amongst us,
we may live out our lives
Challenging and changing
Challenged and changed.

Readings

Exodus 22:21–31 *Community and hospitality*

1 Peter 4:8–9 *Good stewards of God's grace*

3 John 5–8 *Gaius' hospitality*

Prayer Activity

Invite someone new round to your house or take them out for a coffee. Enjoy the conversation and time spent getting to know each other.

Prayer for the Church

Those who attempt to change the Church to make it more congruent with the Gospel and able to meet the challenges of these times

especially the Panel on Review and Reform.

Blessing

Blessed be the sinner who knows their need of God.

Sacrificial/Oppressive Relationships

What of those unhealthy relationships, those times when the life is sapped from you because of oppressive acts and consistent bullying? The Bible is not spared from them. In fact there are too many in amongst the great deeds of God's people. But there they are, beacons for those who suffer with them. And even with God there isn't always a happy ending. These stories break people, sometimes for the better and sometimes for the worst. They spill with the anguish and pain of heaven. And this is indeed heaven, real heaven, down amongst us all, in relationship, in defiance and in longing hope.

SACRIFICIAL/OPPRESSIVE RELATIONSHIPS – JESUS AND JUDAS

Why was this perfume not sold for three hundred denarii and the money given to the poor?

~ John 12:5 ~

Sometimes I just can't keep up with you, Jesus.
One minute you talk about the poor,
the next you talk of banquets and feasting.
One minute you tell the rich young man to give up everything,
and the next you are producing more wine for the wedding.
One minute you said there will be poor with us always
and the next you are being bathed in expensive oil.

But then, maybe these moments call me to see beyond:
not seeking an immediate quick fix,
but living into the future;
not solving a problem by throwing a solution at it,
but choosing to live a more permanent way of justice.

Jesus, help me recognise the sacred moments
that call for a change in my living,
that call for a change in me.
May I now not imagine problem A will be solved with solution B,
or there is a formula to solve all the world's problems,
but that by living more justly,
I may be ready to celebrate goodness and hope when it happens,
knowing each is part of a lifetimes journey,
where I am called to give my whole life
to being an agent for change in the realm of love.

Readings

Mark 9:31–8   *In this for the long term*
Luke 18:18–30   *Giving up*
John 12:1–8   *Jesus anointed at Bethany*

Prayer Activity

Being an agent of change begins with prayer. Tear out stories of injustice from the paper today and paste them into a scrap book or onto a sheet of paper and hold them with you throughout the day and the rest of the week.

Prayer for the Church

Those who enable the celebration of life and faith through the arts and help others by this means to discover their gifts and talents

especially the Netherbow Arts Centre.

Blessing

Celebrate the wonder of God;
celebrate the moments when heaven dances with earth;
celebrate the doorways that set justice free;
and live your life as that celebration, everyday.

OPPRESSIVE/SACRIFICIAL RELATIONSHIPS – STEPHEN AND SAUL

... and the witnesses laid their coats at the feet of a young man named Saul.

~ Acts 7:58 ~

God,
even if I do not always find myself the bearer of eloquent words
that speak out clearly for the sake of justice,
and even if I never find myself
at the front of protests marches in the name of peace,
may you never find me holding the coats.

Even if I cannot shout as loud as my neighbour
in the ears of those who need to know the truth,
and even if I cannot always be singing in protest
for your sake and in the name of your love,
may you never find me holding the coats.

Even if I do not always speak out
on behalf of those who have been silenced by the powerful,
and even if I do always have the words to say
to those who wait to hear,
may you never find me holding the coats.

Instead, if I do not find myself on the frontline like this,
may I encourage with my blessing,
strengthen with my prayers,
nourish hope with my faith,
and hold with my love,
those who do.

Readings

Psalm 23	*The Lord is my shepherd*
John 15:5–10	*Vine and branches*
Act 9:54–60	*The stoning of Stephen*
1 John 3:11–18	*Love one another*

Prayer Activity

Spend some time today searching through the paper or Internet for just one story of someone involved in non-violent protest. Read their story and pray for them and for those who gather round them in support and witness.

Prayer for the Church

Those who today, in the name of the Church and under the guidance of the Gospel, will share their faith through word and action

especially in some local initiative for outreach and evangelism.

Blessing

Listen for the rejoicing of heaven,
each time a word of love is spoken.
Listen for the encouragement of heaven,
each time a throat is cleared.
Listen for the blessing of heaven,
each time the kingdom is made known.

OPPRESSIVE/SACRIFICIAL RELATIONSHIPS – HOSEA AND GOMER

Go, take to yourself a wife of whoredom and have children of whoredom, for the land commits great whoredom by forsaking the LORD.

~ Hosea 1:2 ~

How much it must have hurt Hosea
to live in an unfaithful marriage,
to know his love was not returned,
to live in a relationship that hurt,
yet not be able to give it up.
How much it must have hurt Hosea?
You don't ask folk to live in abusive relationships,
but this story is not about Hosea.
It is about you, O God.
You and us.

Sometimes our love cannot transform the other
and we can only walk away and allow it to repair us.
But Hosea's story is the reflection of your story
and you don't walk away.
Here is a love that never gives up,
cannot give up,
for you
are God and not a human being.

How can we speak of your love,
that alone can live through our abuse,
that remains strong despite the partings,
that hankers after us when we are gone,
and waits steadfastly for us?

With such a love we have no words to speak of it,
so may we simply trust we live within it.

Readings

Hosea 1:1-11   *Hosea's family/Israel's family*
Hosea 11:1-11   *God's steadfast love*
John 15:11-17   *The greatest love*
Romans 8:37-9   *Nothing can separate us*

Prayer Activity

Find a stone or an image of a rock or mountain. Consider how long it has been there, what world crises and events have passed and yet it stands there. Reflect on God's steadfast love: its constancy, permanence and eternalness. Enjoy that truth.

Prayer for the Church

Those who guide, administer and make arrangements for the Church's life at national level

especially the Central Services Committee, Legal Questions Committee, Investments, and the Nomination Committee.

Blessing

Live the day in love:
speak of it;
walk through it;
trust in it;
and know you live in God.

Unconditional Relationships

A father looks and longs for his son to come home – even when that son left home selfishly head-strong; a daughter-in-law stays by her mother-in-law's side – even though she is not duty bound and this more difficult life choice will gain her nothing; and a brother, plotted against and sold into slavery by jealous siblings, forgives and reconciles his whole family. These are the great stories of the Bible, the great stories of love – love that asks for nothing in return but loves anyway. And although we find that unconditional way so difficult to put into practice, when we can give or receive that kind of love, everything makes sense; Christ is present, faith is strong and life is worth living.

UNCONDITIONAL RELATIONSHIPS –
PRODIGAL SON AND FATHER

*… let us eat and celebrate; for this son of mine was dead and is alive again;
he was lost and is found!*

~ Luke 15:23–24 ~

Father God,
For giving me more than my share,
For allowing me to go my own way,
For letting me be my own person,
Thank you.

Yet in independence,
when my world has chaos all around,
when I have made bad choices
and have nothing and no one to turn to,
Even when others ask why you do,
Thank you for waiting for me.
Even when I think I know best,
And lose myself, thank you for finding me.

Thank you, that though I feel far from home,
You are never distant,
Though I close off and focus on other things,
You are always open and unconditional in your embrace.
Though I am 'prodigal',
you are,
unyieldingly,
love.

Readings

Galatians 3:23–9 *All children of God*
Matthew 8:1–4 *Asking for what we need*

Prayer Activity

The word 'prodigal' has come to be thought of as a negative term for someone who is 'long lost' or misguided and off the straight and narrow. However, 'prodigal' really means 'lavish' or 'extravagant' and whilst this can be seen from a negative perspective in terms of the son in the story, in terms of the prodigal father there is a much more positive understanding. Think of the 'prodigal' aspects of your life and hold both negative and positive feelings before God.

Prayer for the Church

Those who guide the Church in temporal matters and ensure that in its dealings that justice prevails

especially the Law Department.

Blessing

God of extravagant love,
Of outstretched arms,
Meet with us now,
And welcome us home.

UNCONDITIONAL RELATIONSHIPS – RUTH AND NAOMI

So the two of them went on until they came to Bethlehem. When they came to Bethlehem, the whole town was stirred because of them.

~ Ruth 1:19 ~

God, today we remember that
In a time when women only had status through men,
In a land where journeys were always long and tiring
And in circumstances that were risky and unconventional
Ruth clung to Naomi in loyal love.

And with the gleaning of a harvest,
And the reciprocated concern of Naomi,
A new bond was made and a new family begun.

So now we affirm families of our time:
For those bound by action not blood,
For those not recognised by some but admired by others,
For those trying to fit and live up to expectations,
For those journeying through tragedy gleaning something of a future.

Loving God,
By the telling of the story of Ruth and Naomi,
Teach us whom we should stand beside and cling to with devotion.
May all the bonds of love you forge in us be strengthened,
For this is your unexpected,
unconventional,
unconditional way that stirs us and moves the world.

Readings

Luke 8:42–8   *Faith makes a woman well*
Psalm 22:1–11   *Trusting God*

Prayer Activity

There was of course another 'Bethlehem story' – read the Christmas story and consider the people and the family there, reflecting on the unconventional and unconditional aspects you recognise and relate to.

Prayer for the Church

Readers, elders and all local church leaders, and those who provide training for them and all Christian people as they seek to grow in faith, prayer and service.

Blessing

May the God of Ruth and Naomi
bind us together with ties of love and loyalty
and may the peace of Christ unite us in hope and joy.   AMEN.

UNCONDITIONAL RELATIONSHIPS – JOSEPH AND HIS FAMILY

And he kissed all his brothers and wept upon them; and after that his brothers talked with him.

~ Genesis 45:15 ~

God,
in Jacob, you show us – love that has favourites breads jealousy
in Joseph, you remind us – vision without sensitivity creates misunderstanding
in the brothers, you teach us – that wrong turns need righting.

God, your love story is not hearts and flowers
Not idyllic and easy.
Your love story is:
slow but sure
watching and waiting,
enduring and exciting.
Your story is life and death,
Birth and grief,
Cross and tomb,
Full and constant.

Unconditional God,
thank you for the opportunities that people will have today,
to talk things through,
to meet again after time apart,
to draw lines under grudges and let go of bitterness.
Thank you for the healing moments where people can:
Weep in remorse,
Sigh in relief,
Relax in relationships
smile at new people
and feel known and loved – loved and known by you.   AMEN

Readings

Genesis 45   *A reconciliation*
John 4   *A woman known and loved*

Prayer activity

Thinking of Joseph and his family, is there anyone in your family or circle of friends that you have not spoken to for a long time? Why is this? Is there any hurt or past regret? Hold this before God and ask for the grace to make moves of reconciliation and restoration.

Prayer for the Church

Our own part in the Church and the special and unique gifts I have been given by God to contribute to the building up of the body of Christ.

Blessing

Let the love story of the Creator
the healing of the Saviour
and the enthusiasm of the Spirit
shine in you this day,
for all the world. AMEN.

Daily Bible Readings

The asterisk* denotes the following Sunday's readings and psalm prescribed in the Revised Common Lectionary (and as in Common Order*), or the readings set for special festivals.*

These readings come from the Australian Publication, *With Love to the World*, a daily Bible reading guide used throughout Australia and increasingly world-wide. It contains short notes on each passage by writers who are knowledgeable about the biblical background. It is published quarterly and copies can be ordered through the Church of Scotland's Office of Worship and Doctrine (see Acknowledgements page). The likely annual subscription would be £10.

NOVEMBER 2007			Sun	9	Psalm 72:1–19 (1–7, 18–19*)
Mon	26	Romans 13:11–14*			
Tue	27	Amos 5:14–22			
Wed	28	Matthew 24:1–14	Mon	10	Matthew 11:2–11*
Thu	29	Matthew 24:36–44*	Tue	11	1 Thessalonians 2:13–20
Fri	30	Matthew 24:45–51	Wed	12	Job 1:6–28
			Thu	13	James 5:7–11 (7–10*)
DECEMBER 2007			Fri	14	Revelation 2:8–11
Sat	1	Isaiah 2:1–8*	Sat	15	Isaiah 35:1–10*
Sun	2	Psalm 122*	Sun	16	Psalm 146:5–10*
Mon	3	Romans 15:4–13*	Mon	17	Matthew 1:1–17
Tue	4	2 Kings 1:2–17	Tue	18	Matthew 1:18–25*
Wed	5	Matthew 3:1–12*	Wed	19	Matthew 1:26–38
Thu	6	John 8:31–47	Thu	20	Romans 1:1–7*
Fri	7	John 8:48–58	Fri	21	Isaiah 7:1–9
Sat	8	Isaiah 11:1–10*	Sat	22	Isaiah 7:10–16*

Sun	23	Psalm 80:1–7, 17–19*
Mon	24	Isaiah 63:7–9*
Tue	25	Psalm 148*
Wed	26	Titus 2:11–14
Thu	27	Hebrews 2:10–18*
Fri	28	Luke 2:1–7
Sat	29	Luke 2:8–14 (1–20*)
Sun	30	Matthew 2:13–23*
Mon	31	Psalm 96

JANUARY 2008

Tue	1	Luke 2:15–21
Wed	2	Jeremiah 31:7–14
Thu	3	John 1:10–18*
Fri	4	Ephesians 1:3–14*
Sat	5	Matthew 9:14–17
Sun	6	Psalm 147:12–20*
Mon	7	Matthew 3:13–17*
Tue	8	Acts 10:34–43*
Wed	9	Colossians 1:24–2:5
Thu	10	Ephesians 3:1–12
Fri	11	Isaiah 49:8–16a
Sat	12	Isaiah 42:1–9
Sun	13	Psalm 29*
Mon	14	Revelation 22:1–5
Tue	15	John 1:29–42*
Wed	16	1 John 2:18–25
Thu	17	1 Corinthians 1:1–9*
Fri	18	2 Peter 1:1–11
Sat	19	Isaiah 49:1–7*
Sun	20	Psalm 40:1–11*
Mon	21	Matthew 4:12–17
Tue	22	Matthew 4:18–25 (12–23*)
Wed	23	1 Corinthians 1:10–18*

Thu	24	Amos 3:1–8
Fri	25	Isaiah 8:18–22
Sat	26	Isaiah 9:1–4*
Sun	27	Psalm 27:1–9 (1, 4–9*)
Mon	28	Matthew 5:1–12*
Tue	29	1 Corinthians 1:18–31*
Wed	30	1 Corinthians 4:8–13
Thu	31	Zephaniah 2:3, 3:11–13

FEBRUARY 2008

Fri	1	Psalm 37: 1–11
Sat	2	Micah 6:1–8*
Sun	3	Psalm 15*
Mon	4	Isaiah 58:1–9a
Tue	5	1 Corinthians 2:1–12
Wed	6	Matthew 5:13–20
Thu	7	Matthew 17:1–9*
Fri	8	2 Peter 1:16–21*
Sat	9	Exodus 24:12–18*
Sun	10	Psalm 2*
Mon	11	Romans 5:12–19*
Tue	12	Matthew 6:1–6, 16–21
Wed	13	1 Corinthians 9:24–7
Thu	14	Matthew 4:1–11*
Fri	15	Genesis 2:4–7, 15–20a
Sat	16	Genesis 2:20b–3:7 (2:15–17; 3:1–7*)
Sun	17	Psalm 32*
Mon	18	Matthew 20:17–28
Tue	19	John 3:1–17*
Wed	20	Acts 8:1–13
Thu	21	Romans 4:1–5, 13–17*
Fri	22	James 2:20–6
Sat	23	Genesis 12:1–9 (1–4a*)
Sun	24	Psalm 121*

Mon	25	Romans 5:1–11*
Tue	26	John 4:5–15 (5–42*)
Wed	27	John 4:16–26
Thu	28	John 4:27–42
Fri	29	Isaiah 42: 14–21

MARCH 2008

Sat	1	Exodus 17:1–7*
Sun	2	Psalm 95*
Mon	3	John 9:1–12
Tue	4	John 9:13–34 (1–41*)
Wed	5	Ephesians 5:8–14*
Thu	6	John 8:12–20
Fri	7	1 Samuel 16:1–13*
Sat	8	Psalm 23*
Sun	9	John 11:1–16 (1–45*)
Mon	10	John 11:17–32
Tue	11	John 11:33–45
Wed	12	Psalm 116: 1–9
Thu	13	Romans 8:6–11*
Fri	14	Ezekiel 37:1–14*
Sat	15	Psalm 130*
Sun	16	Isaiah 50:4–9a*
Mon	17	Philippians 2:5–11*
Tue	18	Matthew 21:1–11
Wed	19	Matthew 26:1–5, 14–16 (26:14–27:66*)
Thu	20	Matthew 26:31–46
Fri	21	Matthew 26:47–68
Sat	22	Psalm 31:9–16*
Sun	23	Colossians 3:1–4*
Mon	24	Matthew 26:69–27:10
Tue	25	Matthew 27:11–31
Wed	26	1 Corinthians 11:23–6
Thu	27	Matthew 27:32–54
Fri	28	Psalm 118:1–2, 14–24*

Sat	29	Matthew 28:1–10*
Sun	30	John 20:10–18
Mon	31	John 20:19–31*

APRIL 2008

Tue	1	Matthew 28:11–20
Wed	2	Isaiah 43:1–12
Thu	3	1 Peter 1:3–9*
Fri	4	Acts 2:14a, 24–32*
Sat	5	Psalm 16*
Sun	6	Acts 2:14a, 36–41*
Mon	7	Ezekiel 12:21–8
Tue	8	1 Peter 1:17–23*
Wed	9	2 Peter 3:14–18
Thu	10	Daniel 3:13–35
Fri	11	Luke 24:13–35*
Sat	12	Psalm 116:1–4, 12–19*
Sun	13	Isaiah 33:10–16
Mon	14	Acts 2:42–47*
Tue	15	Nehemiah 9:6–15
Wed	16	1 Peter 2:19–25*
Thu	17	Hebrews 13:17–21
Fri	18	John 10:1–10*
Sat	19	Psalm 23
Sun	20	Acts 6:1–7
Mon	21	Acts 7:55–60*
Tue	22	1 Peter 2:2–10*
Wed	23	Isaiah 28:9–17
Thu	24	John 14:1–14*
Fri	25	Isaiah 8:11–20
Sat	26	Psalm 31:1–5, 15–16*
Sun	27	Jeremiah 29:1, 4–13
Mon	28	Acts 8:5–17
Tue	29	Acts 17:22–31*
Wed	30	1 Peter 3:13–22*

MAY 2008

Thu	1	John 14:15–21*
Fri	2	Isaiah 41:17–20
Sat	3	Psalm 66:8–20*
Sun	4	John17:1–11*
Mon	5	1 Peter 4:12–14, 5:6–11*
Tue	6	2 Corinthians 11:19–31
Wed	7	Luke 24:44–52
Thu	8	Acts 1:1–5
Fri	9	Acts 1:6–14*
Sat	10	Psalm 68:1–10, 32–5*
Sun	11	John 7:37–9
Mon	12	John 20:19–23*
Tue	13	Acts 2:1–11 (1–21)
Wed	14	Acts 2:12–21
Thu	15	1 Corinthians 12:3b–13*
Fri	16	Numbers 11:24–30
Sat	17	Psalm 104:24–35 (24–34, 35b*)
Sun	18	Deuteronomy 4:32–40
Mon	19	Numbers 6:22–7
Tue	20	2 Corinthians 13:11–13*
Wed	21	Matthew 28:16–20*
Thu	22	Genesis 1:1–25 (1:1–2:4a*)
Fri	23	Genesis 1:26–2:4a
Sat	24	Psalm 8*
Sun	25	Genesis 6:9–7:1 (6:9–22, 7:24, 8:14–19*)
Mon	26	Genesis 7:24, 8:14–22
Tue	27	Psalm 46*
Wed	28	Romans 1:1–17 (1:16–17, 3:22b–28 (29–31)*)
Thu	29	Romans 3:21–31
Fri	30	Matthew 7:21–9*
Sat	31	Matthew 8:5–13

JUNE 2008

Sun	1	Matthew 9:1–13 (9–13, 18–26*)
Mon	2	Matthew 9:18–26
Tue	3	Genesis 12:1–9*
Wed	4	Genesis 12:10–13:1
Thu	5	Romans 4:1–12
Fri	6	Romans 4:13–25*
Sat	7	Psalm 33 (1–12*)
Sun	8	Romans 5:1–11 (1–8*)
Mon	9	Romans 5:12–14, 18–21
Tue	10	Matthew 9:35–10:8*
Wed	11	Matthew 10:9–23
Thu	12	Genesis 16:1–15
Fri	13	Genesis 18:1–15*
Sat	14	Psalm 116:1–2, 12–19*
Sun	15	Genesis 21:1–7
Mon	16	Genesis 21:8–21*
Tue	17	Matthew 10:24–31 (24–39*)
Wed	18	Matthew 10:32–9
Thu	19	Romans 6:1–4 (1b–11*)
Fri	20	Romans 6:5–11
Sat	21	Psalm 86:1–17 (1–10, 16–17*)
Sun	22	Genesis 22:1–19 (1–14*)
Mon	23	Genesis 23:1–20
Tue	24	Romans 6:12–19 (12–23*)
Wed	25	Romans 6:20–3
Thu	26	Matthew 10:40–2*
Fri	27	Matthew 11:1–15
Sat	28	Psalm 13*
Sun	29	Matthew 11:16–24 (16–19, 25–30*)
Mon	30	Matthew 11:25–30

JULY 2008

Tue	1	Genesis 24:34–49 (34–8, 42–9, 58–67*)
Wed	2	Genesis 24:50–67
Thu	3	Song of Solomon 2:8–13* (or Psalm 45:10–17*)
Fri	4	Romans 7:1–13 (15–25a*)
Sat	5	Romans 7:14–25a
Sun	6	Romans 7:25b–8:8 (8:1–11*)
Mon	7	Romans 8:9–11
Tue	8	Matthew 13:1–9, 18–23*
Wed	9	Matthew 13:10–17
Thu	10	Genesis 25:19–34*
Fri	11	Genesis 26:34–5, 27:5–10, 30–8
Sat	12	Psalm 119:1:5–12* or Psalm 119:1–8*
Sun	13	Genesis 27:41–28:5
Mon	14	Genesis 28:10–22 (10–19a*)
Tue	15	Romans 8:12–17 (12–25*)
Wed	16	Romans 8:18–25
Thu	17	Matthew 13:24–30 (24–30, 36–43*)
Fri	18	Matthew 13:36–43
Sat	19	Psalm 139:1–12, 23–4*
Sun	20	Matthew 13:31–5, 44–52 (31–3, 44–52*)
Mon	21	Matthew 13:53–8
Tue	22	Genesis 29:1–14
Wed	23	Genesis 29:15–32, 30:22–4 (29:15–28*)
Thu	24	Romans 8:26–30 (26–39*)
Fri	25	Romans 8:31–9
Sat	26	Psalm 105:1–11, 45b* or Psalm 128*
Sun	27	Romans 9:1–13 (1–5*)
Mon	28	Romans 9:14–24, 30–2
Tue	29	Genesis 32:9–12, 22–31 (22–31*)
Wed	30	Genesis 33:1–4, 35:1, 5–15
Thu	31	Matthew 14:1–12

AUGUST 2008

Fri	1	Matthew 14:13–21*
Sat	2	Psalm 17:1–15 (1–7, 15*)
Sun	3	Matthew 14:22–36 (22–33*)
Mon	4	Matthew 15:1–9
Tue	5	Genesis 37:1–4, 12–28*
Wed	6	Genesis 41:14–16, 29–30, 33–6, 39–43
Thu	7	Romans 10:1–13 (5–15*)
Fri	8	Romans 10:14–21
Sat	9	Psalm 105:1–6, 16–22, 45b*
Sun	10	Romans 11:1–2a, 11–24 (1–2a, 29–32*)
Mon	11	Romans 11:25–36
Tue	12	Genesis 41:46–9, 53–4: 42:1–8
Wed	13	Genesis 45:1–15*
Thu	14	Matthew 15:7–20 (10–20, 21–8*)
Fri	15	Matthew 15:21–31
Sat	16	Psalm 133*
Sun	17	Matthew 16:1–12
Mon	18	Matthew 16:13–20*
Tue	19	Genesis 45:16–46:5
Wed	20	Genesis 50:1–3, 15–26
Thu	21	Exodus 1:8–2:10*
Fri	22	Romans 12:1–8*
Sat	23	Psalm 124*
Sun	24	Romans 12:9–21*

Mon	25	Romans 13:1–7
Tue	26	Exodus 2:11–25
Wed	27	Exodus 3:1–15*
Thu	28	Matthew 16:21–8*
Fri	29	Matthew 17:1–2, 14–22
Sat	30	Psalm 105:1–6, 23–6, 45c*
Sun	31	Matthew 18:1–9

SEPTEMBER 2008

Mon	1	Matthew 18:10–20 (15–20*)
Tue	2	Romans 13:8–14
Wed	3	Exodus 4:1–5, 10–17, 27–31
Thu	4	Exodus 5:1–9
Fri	5	Exodus 11:10–12:14 (12:1–14*)
Sat	6	Psalm 149*
Sun	7	Exodus 13:17–14:14
Mon	8	Exodus 14:19–31*
Tue	9	Exodus 15:1b–11, 20–1
Wed	10	Romans 14:1–12*
Thu	11	Romans 15:1–13
Fri	12	Matthew 18:21–35*
Sat	13	Psalm 114*
Sun	14	Matthew 19:13–30
Mon	15	Matthew 20:1–16*
Tue	16	Matthew 20:17–34
Wed	17	Exodus 15:22–16:15 (16:2–15*)
Thu	18	Philippians 1:1–20
Fri	19	Philippians 1:21–30*
Sat	20	Psalm 107:1–9
Sun	21	Philippians 2:1–11 (1–13*)
Mon	22	Philippians 2:12–3:1a
Tue	23	Matthew 21:12–22
Wed	24	Matthew 21:23–32*
Thu	25	Exodus 16:16–35
Fri	26	Exodus 17:1–13 (1–7*)

Sat	27	Psalm 78: 1–4, 12–16*
Sun	28	Exodus 18:1, 10–27
Mon	29	Exodus 19:1–25
Tue	30	Exodus 20:1–4, 7–9, 12–20*

OCTOBER 2008

Wed	1	Matthew 21:33–46*
Thu	2	Philippians 3:1b–11 (4b–14*)
Fri	3	Philippians 3:12–21
Sat	4	Psalm 19*
Sun	5	Philippians 4:1–9*
Mon	6	Philippians 4:10–23
Tue	7	Matthew 22:1–14*
Wed	8	Exodus 30:22–31:11
Thu	9	Exodus 32:1–14*
Fri	10	Exodus 32:15–35
Sat	11	Psalm 106:1–6, 19–23, 43–8 (1–6, 19–23*)
Sun	12	Exodus 33:1–11
Mon	13	Exodus 33:12–23*
Tue	14	Exodus 34:1–9, 29–35
Wed	15	1 Thessalonians 1:1–10*
Thu	16	Matthew 22:15–22*
Fri	17	Matthew 22:23–33
Sat	18	Psalm 99*
Sun	19	Matthew 22:34–46*
Mon	20	1 Thessalonians 2:1–8*
Tue	21	Exodus 40:1–16, 34–8
Wed	22	Deuteronomy 33:44–52
Thu	23	Deuteronomy 34:1–12*
Fri	24	Psalm 90:1–12 (1–6, 13–17*)
Sat	25	Psalm 90:13–17
Sun	26	Joshua 1:1–13, 2:1–14

Mon	27	Joshua 3:1–17 (7–17*)
Tue	28	I Thessalonians 2:9–16
		(9–13*)
Wed	29	Matthew 23:1–12*
Thu	30	Matthew 5:1–12
Fri	31	Revelation 7:9–17

November 2008

Sat	1	Psalm 34:1–22 (1–10, 22*)
Sun	2	Matthew 24:32–45

Mon	3	Matthew 25:1–13*
Tue	4	I Thessalonians 2:17–3:13
Wed	5	I Thessalonians 4:1–18
		(13–18*)
Thu	6	Joshua 6:1–5, 15–16, 20–5
Fri	7	Joshua 24:1–3a, 14–31
		(1–3a, 14–25*)
Sat	8	Psalm 96*
Sun	9	Judges 2:7–23

Mon	10	Judges 4:1–9a, 14–23 (1–7*)
Tue	11	Psalm 123*
Wed	12	I Thessalonians 5:1–11*

Thu	13	I Thessalonians 5:12–28
Fri	14	Matthew 25:14–30*
Sat	15	Zephaniah 1:7, 12–18
Sun	16	Matthew 25:31–40
		(31–46*)

Mon	17	Matthew 25:41–6
Tue	18	Ezekiel 34:1–16 (11–16,
		20–4*)
Wed	19	Ezekiel 34:17–31
Thu	20	Psalm 98
Fri	21	Ephesians 1:15–23*
Sat	22	Psalm 100*
Sun	23	I Corinthians 1:1–3
		(Christ the King)

Mon	24	I Corinthians 1:4–9 (3–9*)
Tue	25	Mark 13:24–31
Wed	26	Mark 13:32–7 (24–37*)
Thu	27	Isaiah 63:15–19
Fri	28	Isaiah 64:1–9*
Sat	29	Psalm 80:1–7, 17–19*
Sun	30	2 Peter 3:1–7
		(first Sunday of Advent)

Serving Overseas with the Church of Scotland
with their families
(to be added to the Prayer for the Church for each day)

Day 1   MALAWI: Andy and Felicity Gaston with Katy and Daniel
Day 2   MALAWI: Helen Scott
Day 3   ZAMBIA: Colin Johnston
Day 4   ZAMBIA: Jenny Featherstone
Day 5   FRANCE: Alan and Lucie Miller with Jacob and Barnabas
Day 6   ISRAEL: Antony and Darya Short, with Joelle and Ezra
Day 7   TRINIDAD: John and Claudette Bacchas with Kerri-Ann and Shena-Marie
Day 8   ISRAEL: Jane and Ian Barron
Day 9   ISRAEL AND PALESTINE: Jeneffer Zielinski
Day 10   BANGLADESH: David and Sarah Hall with Rebecca
Day 11   BANGLADESH: Helen Brannam
Day 12   BANGLADESH: James Pender
Day 13   SRI LANKA: John and Patricia Purves
Day 14   BERMUDA: Alan and Elizabeth Garrity
Day 15   BAHAMAS: Scott and Anita Kirkland with Priscilla and Sarah
Day 16   COSTA DEL SOL: John and Jeannie Shedden
Day 17   ROTTERDAM: Robert and Lesley-Ann Calvert with Simeon, Zoe, Benjamin and Daniel
Day 18   ROME: William and Jean McCulloch with Jennifer
Day 19   AMSTERDAM: John and Gillian Cowie with Matthew, Sarah and Ruth
Day 20   LAUSANNE: Melvyn and Doreen Wood with Calum
Day 21   GIBRALTAR: Stewart and Larisa Lamont
Day 22   GENEVA: Ian and Roberta Manson with Andrew, Robert and David
Day 23   BRUSSELS: Andrew and Julie Gardner, with Bethany and Karalyn
Day 24   MALTA: David and Jacky Morris
Day 25   BAHAMAS: Terry and Virginia Purvis-Smith
Day 26   PORTUGAL: William and Maureen Ross
Day 27   HUNGARY: Aaron and Edit Stevens with Abel and Daniel

Acknowledgements

Scriptural quotations, unless otherwise stated, are from the *New Revised Standard Version,* © 1989 Division of Christian Education of the National Council of the Churches of Christ in the United States of America, published by Oxford University Press.

The blessings at the conclusion of each day, whose sources are given, are reproduced by permission.

The list of Daily Bible Readings is from *With Love to the World* and is reproduced by kind permission.

Pray Now 2008 was prepared by members of the Pray Now Group: Gayle Taylor, Roddy Hamilton, Owain Jones and Fiona Fidgin.

For further information about *Pray Now* and other publications from the Office for Worship and Doctrine, contact:

Office for Worship and Doctrine
Mission and Discipleship Council
Church of Scotland
121 George Street
Edinburgh EH2 4YN
Tel: 0131 225 5722 ext. 359
Fax: 0131 220 3113
e-mail: wordoc@cofscotland.org.uk

We gratefully acknowledge the following for their kind permission to reproduce the pictures used in this book: Bill Kean, Gayle Taylor and Roddy Hamilton.

Music on Tracks 2, 3 and 4 of the CD recording: 'Lies, Damned Lies' and 'As I Went Down'. Written, produced and recorded by Steve Butler, Dot Reid and Charlie Irvine. Owned and published by Sticky Music and available from www.stickymusic.co.uk

Music on Tracks 1, 5, 6, 7 and 8 © Simon Jones.
Produced by Simon Jones [www.simonjonesmedia.com].